The Kingswood School Library

Accession No.			
		160 96	
Name	**Form**	**Date taken out**	**Return date**
Chloe Harper	8 IG	26/1	- 9 FEB 2005
12 June 2012			
29 June 2012			

EATING DISORDERS

Jo Whelan

HODDER
Wayland

an imprint of Hodder Children's Books

White-Thomson Publishing Ltd,
2-3 St Andrew's Place,
Lewes, East Sussex BN7 1UP

Published in Great Britain in 2001 by Hodder Wayland, an imprint of Hodder Children's Books

This book was produced for White-Thomson Publishing Ltd by Ruth Nason.

Design: Carole Binding
Picture research: Glass Onion Pictures

British Library Cataloguing in Publication Data
Whelan, Jo
    Eating Disorders. - (Health Issues)
    1. Eating Disorders - Juvenile literature
    I. Title
    616.8'526

ISBN 0 7502 3178 5

Printed in Italy by G. Canale & C.S.p.A.

Hodder Children's Books
A division of Hodder Headline Limited
338 Euston Road, London NW1 3BH

Acknowledgements
The author and publishers thank the following for their permission to reproduce photographs and illustrations: Associated Press: pages 22 (NBC), 47; Camera Press: page 29; Martyn F. Chillmaid: page 40; Corbis Images: pages 6 (Richard T. Nowitz), 8 (Cydney Conger), 9 (RNT Productions), 11 (Paul A. Souders), 30 (Duomo), 31 (Wartenberg/Picture Press), 32 (Bettmann), 33 (Laura Dwight), 39 (Mitchell Gerber), 45 (Laura Dwight), 48 (Leif Skoogfors), 52 (Richard T. Nowitz); Angela Hampton Family Life Pictures: cover, pages 1, 15, 19, 27, 42, 44, 57, 58; Impact Photos (Oligny/Editing): pages 17, 53; Photofusion: pages 37, 59; Photri-Microstock: page 26; Pictorial Press Ltd: page 25; Popperfoto: pages 21, 34, 43, 50; Science Photo Library: pages 7 (Catherine Pouedras/Eurelios), 16 (Oscar Burriel/Latin Stock), 18 (Alain Dex, Publiphoto Diffusion), 24 (Oscar Burriel), 54 (Ed Young); Topham Picturepoint: page 41; Wayland Picture Library: pages 4, 23, 28, 35, 46. The chart on page 13 is based on one from Health Promotion England, with their permission.

Contents

Introduction
The role of food in our lives

Human beings must eat, or else we die. But the importance of food goes far beyond just keeping ourselves alive. Growing, preparing and eating food is a major part of human culture all around the world.

Preparing food for family and friends is a way of showing love and hospitality. Sitting down to a meal together is not just a cure for hunger but a social occasion.

A get-together

A meal is an occasion for family and friends to get together.

Food also serves a whole range of other purposes:

- as a reward or a bribe
- as a way to offer comfort
- to celebrate special occasions
- to show membership of a religion or culture

Above all, for most people, food is a source of enjoyment. We may not like everything, but in general we enjoy the taste of food, its smell and the texture it makes in the mouth. We don't like being hungry, and eating gives us a feeling of satisfaction. We also know that our bodies need nourishment. Some people take great care to eat a healthy diet, while others don't think about it much. But we think of eating as a healthy and natural part of life.

Treat yourself!
Food is prepared and presented to make an occasion feel special.

A distorted attitude to food

In people with eating disorders, attitudes to food become distorted. They are unable to treat food in a normal way. Instead of being a natural and enjoyable part of life, food becomes an enemy, a weapon, or a best friend. Eating – or not eating – is no longer a response to physical hunger but is driven by emotional needs. For these people, their relationship with food starts to dominate their life, whether they starve themselves or eat uncontrollably.

Attitudes to body shape and weight also become abnormal. Getting and staying thin turn into an obsession, and they develop an intense fear of putting on weight. At the same time, many lose the ability to judge their body size accurately. Even if they are severely underweight, they see their shape as normal or even fat.

What causes eating disorders?

Eating disorders are complex, and there are no simple causes or treatments. However, nearly all doctors agree that they are an expression of underlying emotional problems. Eating, dieting and weight loss become a way of coping with life when a person is unable to deal with problems in a more healthy way. Society's obsession with slimness and physical perfection also plays a part. There may be physical causes such as an imbalance in the brain's messenger chemicals, but this has not yet been proved.

How common are eating disorders?

The major eating disorders are:

- anorexia nervosa
- bulimia nervosa
- compulsive overeating and binge eating disorder

Eating disorders have always been around, but from about the mid-1950s the number of people affected began to increase dramatically. This epidemic was confined to so-called 'Western' societies – such as the rich countries of Europe and North America. These countries share an obsession with slimness alongside a plentiful supply of food. As Western cultural values spread, eating disorders are starting to increase in other regions.

About 90 per cent of those affected by anorexia and bulimia are female, and those in their teens and early 20s are at the highest risk.

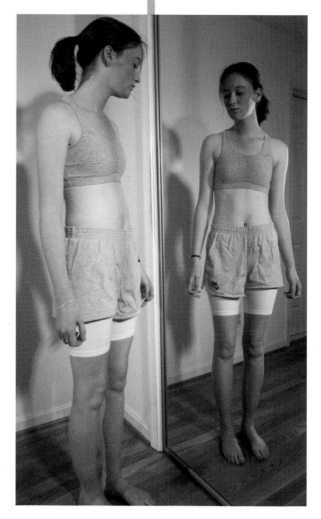

Anorexia
People with anorexia tend to judge their value by looking at their size and weight.

Compulsive overeating and binge eating disorder affect the sexes more equally and are seen in a wider age group.

Today it is estimated that anorexia affects about 1 per cent of teenage girls in the USA. In the UK, over 4,500 new cases are diagnosed every year. Bulimia is more common, affecting 1-3 per cent of young women in the USA and accounting for over 6,500 new cases per year in the UK. Compulsive overeating is the commonest disorder; accurate figures are hard to produce because many people never report the problem.

The impact of eating disorders

It is not surprising that eating disorders often begin in the teenage years, given the rapid physical, emotional and social changes that young people have to deal with at this time. Eating disorders have serious effects on health and cause a great deal of distress to the people affected and their families and friends. They are difficult to understand and hard to overcome. Sufferers and their families often feel helpless and desperate. Both need help from doctors or therapists who are experienced in working with these problems. With professional help, the support of loved ones and hard work from the sufferers themselves, the grip of eating disorders can be broken.

Binge eating
Bingeing means eating an abnormally large amount of food in a short time.

About this book

Chapter 1 looks at what's in food, what makes a good diet and what is a healthy weight. The next three chapters describe the major eating disorders, focusing on their symptoms, effects on the body and psychological impact. Chapter 5 explores the causes of eating disorders, and Chapter 6 looks at treatment. On pages 60-61 there are details of books, Web sites and organizations that offer information and support, and the Glossary on page 62 explains the less familiar terms used in the book.

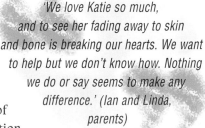

'We love Katie so much, and to see her fading away to skin and bone is breaking our hearts. We want to help but we don't know how. Nothing we do or say seems to make any difference.' (Ian and Linda, parents)

1 Nutrition, weight and diet
Know what's healthy

What is food made of?

The foods we eat are all made up of three types of nutrient: carbohydrates, fats and proteins. They also contain small amounts of minerals and vitamins, and a lot of water. Eating a wide variety of foods is the best way to ensure that your body gets all the nutrients it needs.

Carbohydrates come in two types and are found mainly in plant foods. **Simple carbohydrates** are called sugars and their main function is to provide energy. **Complex carbohydrates** can be either digestible (starch) or indigestible (dietary fibre). Starch is an energy source, and fibre provides bulk to help food move through the intestines easily.

Fats are found in animal foods (meat, eggs and dairy products) and in plants, where they are called oils. They are classified as either **saturated** (most animal fat) or **unsaturated** (most plant oils). Too much saturated fat in the diet is linked to heart disease. Fats and oils have two functions: they are a concentrated source of energy, and they contain fatty acids, which our bodies need for making cell membranes, hormones and the chemicals of the immune system. Fat is also used as a protective coating for the organs, as insulation against the cold, and as an energy store.

Pasta primavera
Fruit and vegetables and starchy foods like pasta should make up the bulk of our diet, so this is a good healthy meal.

Proteins are made up of chemicals called amino acids. They are present in most foods: animal products are the richest source, but there are also good amounts in beans, peas, lentils, grains and nuts. Proteins form the basic structure of our skin, muscle, connective tissue and organs. They also have vital functions in cell repair, hormones and the immune system. Some proteins act as enzymes, which are essential to many of the chemical reactions that take place in the body. Protein can also provide energy, but is only used in this way if other energy sources are not available.

Most of the **minerals** we need are plentiful in a wide range of foods, but we need to be careful that our intake of calcium and iron is sufficient. Calcium is used in bones and teeth, and is especially important for growing children and teenagers. It is found in dairy foods, tinned sardines, whole grains and green vegetables. Iron is part of red blood cells. A shortage means that less oxygen can be

Growing boys

Teenage boys need more food energy in their diet than girls or most adults – but junk food isn't the best way to get it.

carried in the blood, and makes us tired and breathless; this is called anaemia. The best source of iron is meat, and it is also present in dark green vegetables, beans and iron-enriched breakfast cereals. Mineral supplements should be used carefully: many minerals are harmful if too much is taken, and large amounts of one can interfere with the balance of others.

Vitamins are organic (carbon-containing) substances that are essential to healthy bodily functioning. Nobody really knows how much of each vitamin we need to create the best possible state of health. Governments have set out minimum amounts called recommended daily allowances (RDAs). Vitamins A and D are toxic at high doses, and very large amounts of some other vitamins may also be harmful.

Energy

Without energy, our bodies would grind to a halt. It is needed to drive all our physical and chemical processes, as well as to move our muscles and do work. Energy is measured in metric units called joules or imperial units called calories. However, these are very tiny; when people talk about calories in foods they generally mean kilocalories (1 kcal = 1,000 calories). The metric equivalent is kilojoules (kJ).

200 kcal

95 kcal

350 kcal

385 kcal per pint

Calories in food

Different food groups contain different amounts of energy. The richest source of energy is fat/oil at 9 kcal per gram. Carbohydrates and protein contain 4 kcal per gram and alcohol provides 7 kcal per gram.

80 kcal per slice

50 kcal

How much energy do we need?

The amount of energy each person needs in their diet depends on their height, build, age, sex and level of physical activity. Children and teenagers need more energy in proportion to their size than adults. As a rough guide, adult women need around 2,000 kcal per day and teenage girls around 2,200 kcal. The figures for adult men and teenage boys are about 2,500 and 2,800 kcal per day respectively.

All our energy comes from food. The digestive system breaks down nutrients into simple molecules that are carried in the bloodstream and taken in by cells. Inside the cell they go through a series of chemical reactions to release the energy they contain – in much the same way as petrol is burnt to power an engine.

Not all of this energy is used immediately. Some of it is stored in the chemical bonds of fat molecules, ready to be released again when needed. If we take in more energy than we use up, our fat stores increase and we put on weight. If we take in less energy than our body uses, the fat is broken down and burnt and we become thinner and lighter. When all the fat stores are gone, the body starts burning proteins from the muscles, and then from the vital organs, the immune system and elsewhere. By this time, the person is in a state of starvation. Eventually the whole system begins to fail, and without a supply of energy from food, the person will die.

Malnutrition

News pictures from areas hit by famine show the effects on the body of malnutrition and starvation. This child's bloated belly is caused by a lack of protein.

A healthy diet

The key to a healthy diet is to eat a wide variety of foods, including plenty of fruit and vegetables and not too much fat or added sugar. No foods are 'bad' in themselves, as long as the overall diet is healthy. Food is there to be enjoyed, not worried about. For special occasions or meals out it's perfectly OK to relax and eat whatever you fancy. The important thing is to eat a healthy diet most of the time.

SUGARY AND FATTY FOODS *should be kept to a minimum (e.g. one helping a day). Too many could lead to health problems and unhealthy weight gain. Foods in this group include crisps, fizzy drinks, sweets, chocolate, fried foods, pies and burgers. Diet fizzy drinks avoid the sugar problem, but can still rot your teeth because they are very acidic.*

PROTEIN FOODS: *two portions a day will give all the protein you need. Foods in this group are meat, fish, eggs, dairy foods, beans, lentils, nuts and soya products like veggieburgers.*

MILK AND DAIRY FOODS *are sources of calcium and some vitamins, and we need at least one portion a day. Choosing semi-skimmed milk and low-fat yoghurt is a good way of keeping the fat content down.*

STARCHY FOODS *– bread, cereals, potatoes, rice, pasta – should form the main part of each meal, along with vegetables. Use plenty of wholegrains, e.g. wholemeal bread, wholegrain breakfast cereals.*

FRUIT AND VEGETABLES: *at least five portions each day. Fruit juice and tinned or frozen items can all count towards the five. A portion is a good-sized helping, not just a couple of lettuce leaves!*

Healthy weight

People come in all shapes and sizes – it's part of what makes us individuals. Some are tall, some short. Some are naturally stocky, with broad shoulders and hips and well-built limbs, while others have a narrower frame with slender arms and legs. Teenagers' body shape is still changing – people who are gangly in their teens often fill out by their mid-twenties, and those who are plumper may slim down as they gain extra height.

Because everyone's body is different, there is no such thing as an 'ideal' weight. However, doctors have drawn up a system of weight ranges based on height. A chart of this kind is shown here. People in the 'overweight' and 'fat' or 'very fat' categories run an increased risk of

Weight and height

Charts like these were compiled for adults. Teenagers should use them as a general guide only. If you are worried about your weight, get advice from your doctor or school nurse. The dotted line shows how to read the chart.

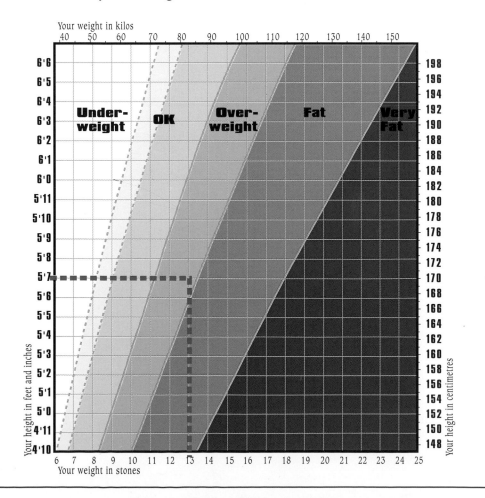

health problems such as diabetes, heart disease and arthritis. For this reason, they should consider losing weight. Being underweight can also cause health problems, or may be a sign of poor health.

Dieting

In the end, 'ideal' weight is a matter of accepting what is realistic and comfortable for you. Some people who would be classed as overweight have decided that their size is part of who they are. They refuse to struggle with diets and reject the social pressure to be slim, preferring to get on and enjoy life without worrying about weight.

Many people, especially women, spend their lives in a constant battle with their weight. In one survey, 66 per cent of female high-school students were on a diet but only 20 per cent of these were actually overweight. Most were dieting to try to conform to media images of the 'perfect' body. We look at this issue in more detail in Chapter 5.

Dieting rarely results in permanent weight loss. Most people gradually put the weight back on, often ending up heavier than they started. They then go on another diet, and the cycle repeats itself. Often the person's self-esteem is tied up with their weight: when they are slim they are happy; when they are heavy they are depressed.

Crash diets

Look in any bookshop and you will see shelves full of books on dieting. Many describe 'wonder-diets' based on ideas such as eating large amounts of grapefruit or eating nothing but protein. Most of these have no scientific evidence to back them up. The diets may be effective, but only because they cut down the amount of energy

Dieting makes you fat!

When we cut back our food intake, the body is programmed to respond as though there was a famine. In order to conserve energy, we begin burning it more slowly. This makes it harder to lose weight. The body also starts burning muscle protein, so some of the weight lost is muscle and not fat. When the person starts eating normally again, more of the energy is converted to fat but the lost muscle is often not fully replaced. So the proportion of fat in the body is higher than it was before the diet.

(calories) eaten. Any diet that uses a very limited range of foods is likely to be harmful, because it will stop you from getting the full range of nutrients. Also, these diets do not help to readjust eating habits, so there is a high chance that any weight lost will be regained.

You may see advertisements for 'miracle' slimming pills – often claiming that you can eat what you like and still lose weight. This isn't true. These products are an expensive waste of money, and some may be harmful. The only way to lose weight is by taking in less energy from food than you use up.

Losing weight sensibly

Teenagers need to be careful about trying to lose weight because they are still growing. A strict diet could stop your body getting the nutrients and energy it needs at this time. If you feel you need to lose weight, get advice from your doctor or school nurse. They can tell you if you really are overweight. If you are, they may refer you to a dietician or specialist nurse who will help you draw up a sensible eating plan. Rather than losing weight, it is often better for teenagers to keep it steady as their height increases, so that they 'grow in' to their weight.

For most people, dieting doesn't work in the long term. Doctors and dieticians agree that the best way to control weight is to eat a healthy diet and take plenty of exercise. Regular exercise is as important as what you eat because it burns up food energy and stops it being stored as fat. If the pattern of healthy eating and exercise becomes part of everyday life, we can achieve and keep a healthy weight without dieting. It helps us look and feel better too!

Shapes and sizes
Differences in body shape help make each of us unique.

2 Anorexia nervosa
More than just dieting

What is anorexia nervosa?

Anorexia nervosa is an illness in which someone deliberately keeps their weight below a healthy level. They achieve this by severely restricting what they eat, and sometimes by vomiting or using laxatives to get rid of meals. 'Anorexia' means loss of appetite, and 'nervosa' means for nervous or psychological reasons. However, this is not an accurate description. Anorexics do not lose their appetite; instead, they deny it, or do not allow themselves to satisfy it.

Distorted view
However thin they become, anorexics often see themselves as too fat.

Doctors have drawn up a set of criteria to define anorexia nervosa:

- ⊛ deliberate weight loss to 85 per cent or less of the healthy minimum for the person's age and height; for growing teenagers or children, deliberate refusal to gain weight at a healthy rate
- ⊛ intense fear of becoming fat, or an intense desire to be thin
- ⊛ a distorted view of their body shape, or measuring their value as a person in terms of their shape or weight
- ⊛ in females, loss of monthly periods for at least three months (usually but not always the case)
- ⊛ the person may or may not use vomiting, laxatives or exercise to get rid of food

Anorexia is not really about eating at all. One doctor describes it as '1 per cent about food, 1 per cent about weight and 98 per cent about the person's inner self, their fears and their feelings of self-worth'.

Who gets it?

Anorexia was described as early as Roman times. Like people in the Western world today, the Romans thought it very important to be slim, even thin. Women would starve themselves to achieve the 'ideal' appearance. After large feasts, men and women would make themselves vomit so that they could eat more without gaining weight. Since about the 1950s, anorexia has been on the increase in Europe, North America and other westernized cultures. It is rarely found in the developing world, except in the wealthy classes.

Like other eating disorders, anorexia is much more common in females. However, about 5-10 per cent of sufferers are male (see page 49). It usually starts in the teenage years. In the USA, it is estimated that 1 per cent of 12-18 year-old girls are affected, with another 5 per cent having a mild form. Certain personality types are especially prone to anorexia, and it is more common among those with high educational achievement. People who get anorexia are often perfectionists who set themselves very high standards. They feel they have to prove themselves by doing

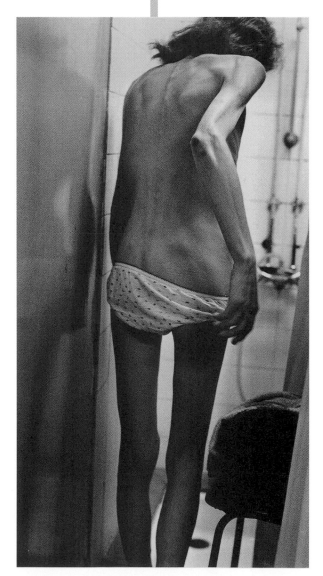

Anorexia
A person with anorexia may eventually look like a victim of starvation.

well at everything and pleasing everybody. They can be very self-critical, and have a tendency to be obsessive about things. Their high levels of willpower and self-control mean they are able to deny themselves food without giving in.

Many come from families with high expectations about behaviour and educational success, or where appearance is seen as very important. The parents are often very protective and closely involved in their children's lives. Conflicts in the family tend to be covered up rather than openly expressed. Sometimes the mother is preoccupied with weight and diet, and passes this anxiety on. However, not all anorexics and their families fit these descriptions. What almost all have in common is low self-esteem. Despite their achievements, deep inside they feel worthless.

'Everyone expected me to carry on getting As, go to a top university, get a good job. I wanted mum and dad and the teachers to be pleased with me, and I put a lot of pressure on myself. Looking back, no one was interested in me, in how I felt about it all. I think anorexia was the only way I could say "This is my life, and I want some control".'
(Lisa, 18)

Setting a standard
Anorexic people often take pride in how well they can control their appetite.

Behaviour and effects

People with anorexia nervosa severely restrict the amount of food they eat, especially the number of calories they take in. They do not eat enough to meet their body's needs, so they lose weight. A growing teenager's weight might stay the same, rather than showing a healthy gain as they get taller.

It often begins like a slimming diet, but anorexics take their food restriction further until their bodies begin to starve. They can lose between 15 and 60 per cent of their bodyweight, so a girl who originally weighed 55 kg might go down to 46 kg or as little as 25-30 kg. They begin to look abnormally thin. The face loses its plumpness so that the cheekbones become prominent. If the weight loss is severe, the ribs and collar bones begin to stand out, and the arms and legs look stick-like.

Eating out
For those with anorexia, eating out with friends becomes something to fear.

Sarah's food diary

When Sarah had anorexia, she kept a diary listing everything she ate each day. Here are some typical entries:
MONDAY: breakfast – glass of skimmed milk, piece of toast; lunch – apple, can of diet drink; evening – two slices of bread (no spread), lettuce and tomato salad, low-fat yoghurt
TUESDAY: breakfast – small bowl of cereal; lunch – sandwich with the filling scraped out, diet yoghurt; evening – two crackers, cottage cheese and an apple
WEDNESDAY: breakfast – glass of skimmed milk; lunch – banana, cereal bar, diet drink; evening – packet of low-calorie soup, two crackers and an orange

People with severe anorexia eat barely enough to survive – perhaps 300-600 kcal per day, compared with the 2,000 or so kcal needed by the average adult woman. When family and friends become worried, they get clever at hiding just how little food they are having. They often lie about what they have eaten, or avoid mealtimes with the excuse that they ate earlier.

Some anorexics eat larger amounts but do not allow their bodies to absorb the food. After eating they deliberately make themselves sick, or take laxatives to try to make the food pass through their body. Others restrict their food intake most of the time but every so often they lose control and binge, then make themselves sick to get rid of what they have eaten. These types of behaviour are called anorexic-bulimic.

People with anorexia sometimes take a lot of exercise, perhaps going for long runs or swims each day. They see this as another way of getting rid of the calories they have eaten.

Effects on the body

As well as severe weight loss, anorexia causes other physical changes and problems. The person has little energy and is often exhausted and weak. They may get faint and dizzy, and often feel cold. Sometimes though, they may have spells of furious activity, cleaning their room, making things or studying for hours. Constipation and stomach pains are common, as are a bloated stomach and swollen face or ankles. Sometimes fine, downy hair called lanugo grows on the body. The hair on the head may begin to fall out.

Premature death

Surveys have shown that 6-10 per cent of people diagnosed with anorexia will die prematurely. About half of these deaths are through suicide, and the rest from the effects of starvation.

Anorexic girls usually find that their periods become irregular or stop altogether. This is caused by a lack of the

Death at 22

In July 1994, Christy Henrich died of anorexia-related complications, at the age of 22. She had been a world-class gymnast, in the United States Gymnastics team.

hormone oestrogen, and can sometimes make it difficult to have children later on. Low oestrogen levels also lead to thinning of the bones (osteoporosis), which can be permanent.

Severe anorexia can lead to a dangerous loss of minerals – called electrolytes – in the body fluids. Calcium, potassium, magnesium and phosphate are essential to the electrical signals that regulate the heartbeat. Starvation, dehydration and vomiting can disrupt the mineral balance and cause irregular heartbeat and even cardiac arrest (when the heart stops beating). The heart muscle itself can shrink and become weak. In extreme cases, these conditions can kill.

Emotional and psychological aspects

People with anorexia become depressed and moody. They feel unable to enjoy life. They are less sociable than before and spend more time alone. When worried friends or family try to talk about their weight or eating habits, they usually insist that nothing is wrong.

They have an overwhelming fear of putting on weight. Eating makes them feel anxious and panicky, so they cut out more and more foods until they are left with a narrow range of items that they feel are 'safe'. Thoughts about food and weight come to dominate their life. Despite hardly eating, they often have a strong interest in cookery and nutrition. They may prepare delicious meals for other people, which they watch them eat but do not share. Sometimes they build up rituals around food, always preparing it in the same way, or cutting it up into tiny pieces.

Mother and daughter

'A Secret Between Friends' is a film from 1996 about a single mother whose daughter has anorexia.

Anorexic people begin to judge themselves almost entirely by how much they weigh. Each kilogram lost is a triumph of their willpower, proof of their ability to control themselves. However, it is never quite enough. One of the most important features of anorexia is a distorted image of the body. No matter how thin they seem to others, most anorexics still see themselves as fat. Nobody knows how or why this distorted picture develops, but it makes it difficult for those affected to accept that they have a problem.

'My friend Janine has got anorexia, but she won't admit it. She keeps going on about how fat she is, but she looks like a skeleton. If you tell her she's too thin, she just says her thighs are fat, or whatever. Everyone wants to be slim, but it's not attractive to be skin and bone like that.'
(Anna, 15)

Anorexia: Carol's story

When Carol was 15 her stepfather started to tease her about her figure, joking that she needed to lose weight. She tried to laugh about it, but secretly she began to worry that he was right. She had never really got used to her new, adult shape, and suddenly her body seemed clumsy and enormous. She felt she would never be attractive – not like the slim, perfect bodies she saw on TV and in magazines. Her self-confidence had always been low, and she began to feel that nothing about her was any good.

She started dieting, and soon lost some weight. Friends started to remark enviously how slim she was, but Carol still felt fat. She set herself a target of losing another 5 kilos, to get rid of the fat on her arms and thighs which she hated so much. She began throwing away her packed lunch on the way to school, then saying to her friends she had already eaten it. In the evenings she stopped eating with the rest of the family, telling her mother she would make her own meals. She spent hours looking at slimming magazines, and soon knew the calorie count of all the different foods. She planned her meals carefully, eating small portions and using lots of 'diet' foods. If she felt she had too many calories one day she would eat even less the next day to make up for it.

Carol felt hungry all the time, but she never gave in. She was proud of how well she could control herself, and with every kilo she lost she felt an exhilarating sense of achievement. Here, at last, was something all her own, something she could control! Deep down she longed to eat more, but was too afraid of putting on weight. And anyway, her legs were still fat. She needed to lose a couple more kilos ...

Magazine images
Fashion photographs in magazines made Carol more unhappy with herself.

3 Bulimia nervosa
A secret disorder

What is bulimia nervosa?

The Greek word 'bulimia' means 'the hunger of an ox', and 'nervosa' means of nervous origin. Bulimia nervosa is an illness in which people eat large amounts of food in a short time, and then get rid of it by purging themselves. Purging is usually by vomiting and/or taking laxatives. Over-exercising and fasting are other ways of compensating for what has been eaten. The uncontrolled eating of large amounts of food is called a binge.

Bingeing and vomiting were common among wealthy Romans and Greeks two thousand years ago. The condition is also mentioned in literature from the eighteenth century, but was not well known until the 1970s. Bulimia nervosa was first recognized as an illness in 1979. Like other eating disorders, it is a sign of underlying emotional problems.

One survey in the USA found that 40 per cent of teenage and college-age girls had binged and then made themselves vomit at least once in their life. However, isolated incidents of this kind are not classed as bulimia. The strict medical definition is that bingeing and purging must happen an average of twice a week or more for at least three months. In severe cases people may do it twice a day, while others only have episodes once or twice a month.

Anorexia and bulimia are closely linked. About half of anorexics also

Eating in private
People with bulimia binge in private, perhaps locking themselves in the bathroom or bedroom.

show some bulimic symptoms, and many bulimia sufferers go through periods of strict dieting between binges. Like those with anorexia, people with bulimia attach great importance to weight and body shape, and have an intense fear of becoming fat and a distorted image of their body.

Life is Sweet
This 1990 film, directed by Mike Leigh, is about a family where the daughter has bulimia.

Who gets it?

Bulimia is most common among women in their late teens and early twenties, though it can occur in younger teenagers, older women and in men. People who develop bulimia have strong ideals about being thin, and tend to judge themselves by their weight and shape. They have usually tried dieting several times but have failed to reach the weight they want.

Many are high achievers who have to cover up their lack of self-confidence at work and in front of friends. Some are prone to depression and other mental health problems. In contrast to anorexics, people with bulimia are often from families where conflicts are strongly expressed. Some feel neglected or rejected by their parents, or have been sexually abused. However, bulimia can affect people from any background. What bulimics have in common is a low sense of their own value, a feeling that they are no good.

Raising awareness

The American Anorexia and Bulimia Association works to increase public awareness about eating disorders. For example, the association has arranged for top model Magali Amadei to tour high schools in the USA, talking to students about her personal experience of bulimia.

Bulimia has been described as a secret disorder. Bingeing and purging take place in private, and the person's weight is usually normal. Close friends, family and even partners may be unaware of the problem, and the affected person is usually too ashamed to talk about it.

Behaviour and effects

At first, eating binges usually happen after a period of strict dieting, when the person is very hungry. But the amount of food eaten goes beyond what they need physically. Bingeing becomes a way of filling emotional emptiness and dealing with feelings of insecurity. Stress, boredom, loneliness, depression, failure or just an unkind word can all trigger a binge.

'I hated my body and I desperately wanted to be thinner. I wouldn't eat anything that was fattening. But when I felt down I craved for something sweet to make me feel better. I'd usually end up giving in, and after I'd eaten it I felt such a failure that I'd go on a binge.'(Katrina, 21)

A binge may bring physical and emotional satisfaction for a while. But feelings of shame and panic soon set in, especially the fear of putting on weight. To get rid of the food, most bulimics make themselves vomit by putting

Binges

When someone binges they lose control over what they eat. Up to half of all binges consist of 600 kcal or less, but they may contain up to 15,000 kcal, eaten in a period lasting between 30 minutes and two hours. The person doesn't usually enjoy the food, or even taste it properly. Binges usually consist of high-carbohydrate foods like bread, cakes, crisps, biscuits and ice cream. If there is nothing else available, people may even resort to eating frozen food. Buying all this food is very expensive.

Purging

After bingeing, people with bulimia make themselves vomit.

their fingers down their throat. Some take vomit-inducing medicines. Others overdose on laxatives to give themselves diarrhoea, thinking that this will stop them absorbing the food. However, 90 per cent of the calories have already been absorbed before the food reaches the bowel, so laxative abuse is ineffective. Even vomiting does not prevent at least 25 per cent of the calories from being absorbed. The reason people with bulimia do not usually become overweight is that they diet between binges. Some do not purge at all but compensate for their binges by starving themselves or taking large amounts of exercise.

Once the pattern is established, the nervous system becomes used to bingeing in certain situations, making it even more difficult to resist. Many doctors believe that bingeing and purging is a kind of addiction, because it can release chemicals called opioids into the brain which bring a short-term sense of pleasure.

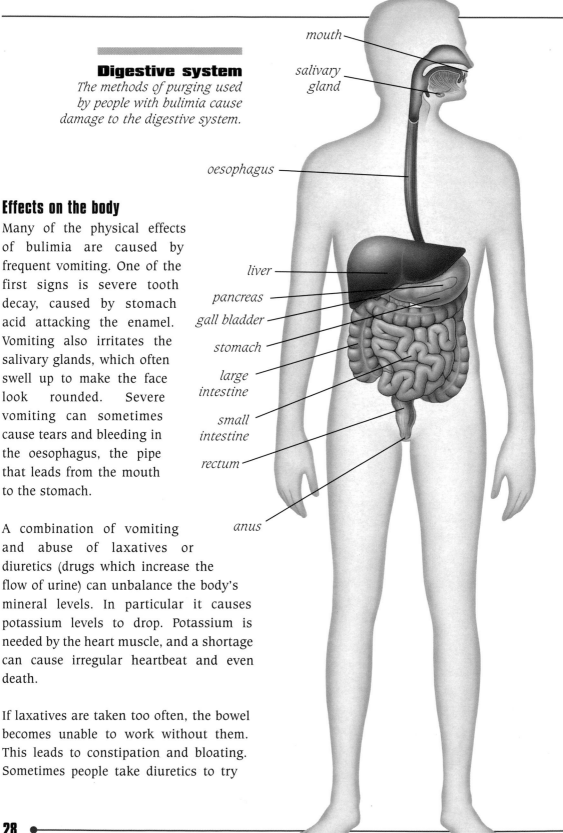

Digestive system

The methods of purging used by people with bulimia cause damage to the digestive system.

mouth

salivary gland

oesophagus

liver

pancreas

gall bladder

stomach

large intestine

small intestine

rectum

anus

Effects on the body

Many of the physical effects of bulimia are caused by frequent vomiting. One of the first signs is severe tooth decay, caused by stomach acid attacking the enamel. Vomiting also irritates the salivary glands, which often swell up to make the face look rounded. Severe vomiting can sometimes cause tears and bleeding in the oesophagus, the pipe that leads from the mouth to the stomach.

A combination of vomiting and abuse of laxatives or diuretics (drugs which increase the flow of urine) can unbalance the body's mineral levels. In particular it causes potassium levels to drop. Potassium is needed by the heart muscle, and a shortage can cause irregular heartbeat and even death.

If laxatives are taken too often, the bowel becomes unable to work without them. This leads to constipation and bloating. Sometimes people take diuretics to try to reduce bloating, but this can cause dangerous dehydration. The bowel usually recovers from laxative damage after a few weeks, but sometimes the problems are permanent.

Very occasionally the stomach becomes so stretched by a binge that it ruptures (splits). This can be fatal.

People with bulimia are generally tired and run down due to poor diet, lack of vitamins and minerals and frequent vomiting. The strain on the body is especially severe if bingeing alternates with stretches of malnutrition caused by very low food intake. Women often find that their periods become irregular. Weight is usually within the normal range but often goes up and down frequently.

Psychological and emotional aspects

People with bulimia often appear outgoing, successful and popular. But underneath, they lack confidence and have a low opinion of themselves. They feel out of control, trapped in a vicious cycle of bingeing and purging. Many hate themselves for their bulimic behaviour, but feel unable to cope without it. Unlike people with anorexia, most realize that they have a problem. However, a few bulimics see the disorder as part of their life and do not feel the need to change.

Speaking out

Diana, Princess of Wales, suffered from bulimia. In 1993 she spoke in public about it, for the first time, at a conference about eating disorders. She said that people with bulimia see it 'as a way of coping, albeit destructively and pointlessly, with a situation they were finding unbearable'.

Chris, a champion wrestler

Chris had been a member of the school wrestling team since he was 15, and had won several medals. Now, at 18, his body was maturing and he was almost too heavy for his old weight class. The next class up was tougher, and Chris worried that he would not make the team. Wrestling was the most important thing in his life – the friendship with his team-mates, the popularity it gave him with girls, the pride at doing something well. Without it he felt he would have nothing, and be no one.

He began dieting to keep his weight down. For a few weeks he stuck to his plan, and lost 2 kilos. But his body cried out for more food, and hunger left him feeling low. One day, when his parents were out, he made his usual sandwich for lunch, trying to ignore

the eggs and bacon in the fridge. Then, as he was eating, something seemed to snap inside his head. He went to the fridge and fried up a couple of eggs and two slices of bacon, then wolfed them down. Before he knew it, he was back at the pan, making more eggs, more bacon, fried tomatoes and six slices of toast. There was cheese in the fridge and he had that too, along with a family-sized bag of crisps. He ate quickly and desperately, hardly tasting the food, conscious only of the hole inside him that demanded to be filled. Finally, after finishing off half a packet of biscuits and a pint of milk, he came to a stop.

His stomach felt tight and stretched, and stood out in a bulge under his T-shirt. He looked at it in panic. Now he'd ruined everything. His diet was a failure, his wrestling career would be wrecked, and he would end up fat and unpopular. He was weak and useless. There was only one thing to do. Chris went to the bathroom, leaned over the toilet and put his fingers in his throat. His stomach was so full that the food came up easily. Afterwards he felt clean and pure.

He began to diet again, but within a week he had another binge. He fell into a pattern, dieting strictly then eating and vomiting when alone in the house. The more he did it, the worse he felt about himself, and the more he turned to binges to fill the emptiness inside him. Nobody knew what was going on, not even the girls he dated. He kept his place in the wrestling team with the help of diuretic drugs, which he took to lose water before weighing sessions. It was only after an unhappy first year at college that he plucked up the courage to see a counsellor about his bulimia.

Looks don't tell
People like Chris may not appear to have any problem.

4 Compulsive overeating
An emotional need

No control
In books and films, someone who can't stop eating may be funny. But compulsive overeating is a serious real-life problem.

What is compulsive overeating?

Eating is called compulsive when it is driven by an urge that the person cannot control. It can be triggered by hunger but is often a response to negative thoughts or feelings. Rather than just satisfying physical hunger, compulsive eating is a way of satisfying emotional needs. It often takes the form of bingeing – that is, eating an abnormally large amount of food in a short time (see page 27). Compulsive bingeing also happens in bulimia. The difference is that compulsive overeaters do not try to get rid of the food afterwards.

Until recently, most people thought that overeaters were just greedy and weak-willed. However, doctors began to realize that the problem was more complex, and in 1994 they defined a condition called binge eating disorder (BED). According to the definition, this involves:

- bingeing an average of at least twice a week for a period of at least six months
- feeling out of control during binges
- feeling upset about the behaviour.

The binges involve at least three of the following:

- eating very quickly
- eating until uncomfortably full
- eating when not physically hungry
- eating alone because of embarrassment about the amount eaten
- feeling disgusted, depressed or very guilty afterwards.

For those affected, BED is just as serious a problem as bulimia or anorexia. Many more people have a problem with compulsive eating but do not meet the BED definition of bingeing twice a week for six months. Some compulsive eaters do not binge at all, but rely on constant snacking, an eating pattern sometimes called 'grazing'.

Some doctors think that compulsive overeating is a form of addiction. Food and eating become like a drug, which the person relies on to take away bad feelings. This is partly psychological and partly physical, because eating causes a temporary increase in serotonin, a brain chemical that helps us feel happy (see page 46).

Grazing
'Grazing' is a habit that can start young.

Eating when not hungry

Few people eat only when they are hungry. Most of us have times when we eat because we are bored, because other people are eating or just because we really want that ice cream or chocolate bar! It's also common to eat for comfort from time to time, and even to binge occasionally. Some people feel guilty about this non-hunger eating, others don't. It is not a serious problem unless it gets out of control and starts to take over your life.

Who gets it?

Compulsive overeating is far more common than anorexia or bulimia. In the USA researchers estimate that 2-5 per cent of the population have binge eating disorder, and many more have a less serious compulsive eating problem. The true numbers are uncertain because most people never seek treatment.

In contrast to other eating disorders, up to half of those affected are male. The majority of people coming for treatment are in their 30s and 40s, but the pattern of overeating often begins in childhood or adolescence. Many have a genetic tendency to be overweight and have been on a series of diets. It is thought that 25-40 per cent of all obese people are compulsive overeaters, and 10-20 per cent have BED. However, not everyone with these disorders is obese or even overweight, because many eat a normal or restricted diet between binges.

Remedial action
These boys in China were given weight-reducing exercises to do during the school holidays.

Compulsive overeaters usually have low self-esteem. They tend to have difficulty in expressing and dealing with their feelings, and may find it hard to form satisfying relationships. Often their lack of self-confidence means they do not stand up for what they want or need, and end up feeling angry and frustrated. People who have suffered sexual abuse have a higher than average risk of developing compulsive overeating, as have people who grew up in families affected by alcoholism or drug addiction.

Behaviour and effects

People who binge usually do it in secret. Some eat junk foods like crisps, biscuits, cakes and chocolates, while others make large quantities of foods like pasta, fried rice or toast. They often eat quickly, without taking time to enjoy the food. Afterwards they usually feel guilty and ashamed, but don't vomit, exercise or use laxatives to purge themselves of the food. Some binge most days, others only a few times a month.

People who overeat by 'grazing' have a constant urge to snack. They might keep biscuits in their desk drawer and chew on one every few minutes, or spend the evening getting through a family pack of crisps.

Compulsive grazing or bingeing often follows a period of dieting. During the diet the person becomes very preoccupied with food, constantly thinking about what they can and can't eat. When they come off the diet they make up for the previous lack of food by starting to overeat. The cause of this reaction might be psychological,

Food for a binge
The food is not chosen because it looks delicious. The person will eat it without stopping to appreciate the taste.

or it might be the body's way of guarding against a future food shortage. The person ends up heavier than they were before, goes on another diet and the cycle repeats itself. This 'yo-yo' dieting can go on for years and can cause great unhappiness.

Effects on the body

Compulsive overeating is bad for health if the person becomes overweight or obese. This puts them at higher risk of heart problems, high blood pressure, diabetes, arthritis and some cancers. Even if weight is normal, a high intake of junk food is low in vitamins, minerals and fibre and leaves less room for healthier foods. Frequent snacking on sweet things causes tooth decay. On rare occasions a very large binge can rupture the stomach or oesophagus (the pipe connecting mouth and stomach); this is very serious and can be fatal.

Psychological and emotional aspects

As we have seen, compulsive eating can sometimes be a physical or psychological reaction to dieting. However, for many people it is triggered by negative feelings such as depression, anxiety, loneliness, emotional pain or frustration. Eating is used as a way of blotting out these feelings rather than facing up to them.

Compulsive overeaters usually feel ashamed and guilty about their eating. This pushes their self-esteem even lower and makes it harder to break free from the pattern. Some share the obsession with weight and thinness that features in anorexia and bulimia, but many do not.

'I come home in the evening and I know I won't see anyone until I go to work again the next day. Weekends are even worse. It's just me and the TV. Food is like a friend. It takes my mind off being lonely and bored. I wish I could control my eating, because I've put on so much weight that I'm embarrassed about meeting people – and that makes me feel even worse.' (Sharon, 25)

CHAPTER 4

Alan tried to blot out his feelings

Alan had always been a plump child. His mother liked to show her love through cooking, and whenever something went wrong she always comforted him with biscuits and sweets. When he started school he was teased about his weight. This knocked his confidence, and he found it difficult to trust people or make friends. Instead of playing with other children he spent more and more time alone, watching TV or playing on his computer. He usually had a few packets of crisps and a fizzy drink to keep him company. He was no good at sport and avoided PE lessons whenever he could. The snacks and lack of exercise meant he piled on even more weight.

When he went to senior school, some older boys began to bully him. With no real friends to stand up for him, Alan became desperately unhappy and his confidence reached an all-time low. To survive the day at school he would eat chocolate when no one was looking, and then biscuits when he got home. His mother noticed how unhappy he was and made sure he always had a big, comforting meal.

His class teacher tried to help him and sent him to the school nurse for advice on losing weight. Alan decided to give it a try, and his mother agreed to help. She stopped buying crisps and biscuits and began to cook healthier meals. But Alan's problems had not gone away, and deep down he thought no one would ever like him, even if he did lose weight. Life seemed hopeless. He started buying even more snacks, and ate them secretly in his room. He knew he should stop, but he couldn't. Eating was the only way to blot out the loneliness and anger he felt inside.

Target for teasing
Alan realized that his classmates were joking about him.

5 What causes eating disorders?
Social, psychological and physical factors

As we have seen, eating disorders are caused by emotional and psychological problems that make a person feel unable to cope with life. In this chapter we will look in more detail at the types of problems and pressures that lead people to resort to eating disorders. We will also examine possible physical factors that might make some people more vulnerable. Anorexia, bulimia and binge eating disorder are closely linked and share many of the same causes. Therefore, most of the topics in this chapter apply to all of them.

People with eating disorders are individuals, and each has their own reasons for behaving in the way they do. Often these reasons are unconscious, so the person cannot put them into words. The causes set out here are the most common. Not everyone with an eating disorder has all or even most of these problems.

'You can never be too rich or too thin,' said Wallis Simpson, who, as Duchess of Windsor, was a stylish figure in high society in the years before and after the Second World War.

There are no 'bad' reasons for developing an eating disorder. They are a response to natural human needs – the need to be accepted by oneself and others, to fit in with the group, to get rid of painful feelings or to deal with pressures that seem overpowering. It is no coincidence that they most often start in the teenage years, when rapid physical, social and emotional changes can cause feelings of anxiety and confusion.

Society, the media and the ideal body

Eating disorders are only common in societies that have plentiful food but place a high value on slimness. This includes North America, Western Europe and other countries that have 'Western' cultural values. In these countries we are constantly bombarded with media images – from television, films, magazines and advertisements – showing the 'ideal' body, especially the female body. These ideal women are tall, beautiful and very, very slim. The images tell us that they are happy, successful and have lots of boyfriends. Women with other body shapes are hardly ever shown, so it is easy to think of these 'ideal' women as normal. In fact, people with ultra-slim bodies and perfect faces are very unusual – and many of them end up working as models, actresses or pop singers! Even most of these rely on dieting to keep their shape, and eating disorders are common in these groups.

In reality women come in all shapes and sizes, and for most of them the 'supermodel' figure just isn't possible. However, many girls and women constantly compare their bodies to this

On show
*The media focus attention
on how celebrities look.*

impossible ideal, and become unhappy when they don't match up. Instead of helping people accept their bodies, society and the media encourage this unhappiness. Celebrities with normal figures are made fun of in newspapers for being 'fat'. Magazines are full of advice on slimming and advertisements for expensive body-toning treatments. At the same time we are exposed to a flood of advertisements for junk foods. Food is available 24 hours a day, wherever we go. For many people, controlling the amount they eat becomes a daily struggle.

Fast food
Thinness is fashionable, but so is eating the fast foods that are available any time, anywhere.

CHAPTER 5

What is the ideal body?

Ideas about an attractive body shape differ from culture to culture and change through history. It was only in the 1960s that Western societies started to become obsessed with slimness. The actress Marilyn Monroe, who came to fame in the 1950s, is seen as one of the greatest sex symbols of all time. Yet her curvy figure was very different from today's film stars. Further back in history, masterpieces by painters such as Rubens feature well-rounded female nudes, who were obviously the beautiful women of their day and are still very much admired. In societies where food is in short supply, being plump is a often a symbol of beauty and wealth, because it shows that the person is well fed.

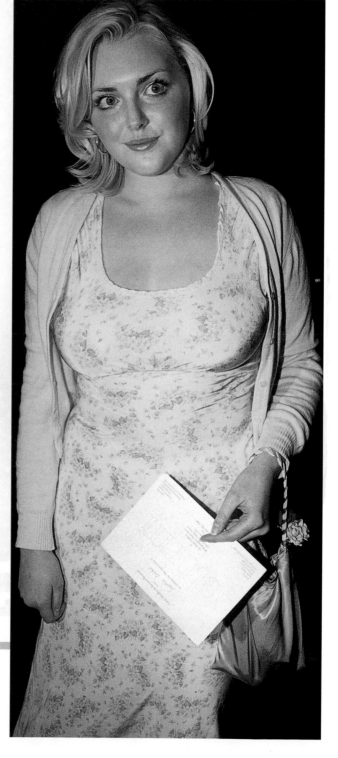

Alternative model

Model Sophie Dahl presents a different image from the ultra-slim supermodels.

Girls learn from a young age that society judges them by how they look. Many come to believe that their lives would improve in all sorts of ways if they could just lose a little weight. For some, their weight and body shape become the main marker by which they value themselves as people. Girls who think this way are vulnerable to eating disorders. Others grow up to spend their lives in a fruitless and unhappy battle with their weight.

These pressures are probably one of the main reasons why eating disorders are much more common in girls and women than in boys and men. Males do worry about their body shape, but this tends to be about how tall or muscular they are rather than how thin. In the past they faced less media pressure to conform to an ideal look, but this is changing. Boys and men are becoming more fashion-conscious and care more about their appearance. The media is portraying more images of cool, successful men with perfectly toned bodies. This may be leading to an increase in eating disorders in males.

Society's obsession with body shape sets the stage for eating disorders, but it is not the whole story. Psychological and emotional factors also play a major role.

Personality

People with eating disorders have very low self-esteem, though many hide this behind an image of success or popularity. They are very sensitive to criticism and failure, so that even a small criticism or mistake makes them think they are useless. They find it hard to deal with stress,

Obsession
Checking your weight can become an obsession.

perhaps because they have not had the support and security they needed in the past. People who develop anorexia are often perfectionists who see anything but the best as a failure. This makes it difficult for them to accept themselves as they are.

Being in control

No matter how much our lives are controlled by others, no one can control what we do to our own bodies. Nobody can make us eat, or – unless they lock us up – stop us from eating too much. Most doctors and therapists believe that the desire to achieve control of our own lives is at the root of many cases of eating disorders, especially anorexia.

For teenagers, everything seems to be changing at once. Their bodies change shape. They become more independent – usually both because they want to and because others expect it. As they start moving towards adulthood they begin to develop a new sense of who they are as a person, and how they relate to others. Relationships with the opposite sex take on a new meaning and arouse strong feelings. On top of this, they are under pressure to do well at school. Some teenagers get very anxious about these changes and feel that their lives are getting out of control.

Some feel unable to express themselves as an independent person because other people – usually their parents – have too much control over their lives. This type of family background is more common in anorexics. Their parents are sometimes over-protective, inflexible and closely involved in their daughter's or son's life. They have high expectations regarding behaviour and schoolwork. The teenager may feel loved because of her success and her good behaviour, rather than for herself.

Stress
Crown Princess Victoria of Sweden suffered from an eating disorder in the late 1990s. It was said to have been brought on by the stress of her increasing public commitments.

In these situations, some people try to get control of their lives by controlling their bodies. Their 'success' in losing weight gives them a sense of achievement and independence. Self-control becomes all-important, a way of holding back the anxiety about other areas of life. Anorexia can also be a way of drawing attention to the person inside. The anorexic person may be saying: 'Look, I am fading away, and you will all be sorry when I am gone.'

Not everyone has the self-control to deny their hunger for long periods. In many cases, bulimia begins when a person loses control of their anorexic behaviour and binges to satisfy their hunger. To try to regain control they get rid of the binge food by vomiting, laxatives or exercise, and go back to their restrictive diet until the cycle repeats itself.

Family problems

Conflicts within the family are often one of the causes of eating disorders. Anorexia is sometimes the result of a

Conflict
Teenagers need a subtle mixture of protection and freedom.

strict and over-protective family, while a lack of interest from parents can contribute to bulimia. People from families where there is alcoholism or drug abuse are more prone to bulimia than others. Sometimes people develop eating disorders because they have been sexually abused.

Mothers who are constantly dieting can pass their anxiety about body shape to their children, especially daughters.

Not wanting to grow up

For some people, anorexia is an attempt to stop the process of growing up. The person may be aware that this is what they are doing, or it may be unconscious. An anorexic girl loses her feminine shape, her breasts shrink and her periods usually stop. A boy will not develop adult muscle cover. Making the body child-like again is a way of dealing with the anxieties that come with growing up.

Someone who has been sexually abused may try to stop their body developing because they are ashamed of it, or because they do not want to attract sexual attention. People who have been teased because they were early developers also run an increased risk of eating disorders.

Growing up
Turning from a child into an adult is a stressful experience, provoking many different feelings.

Stressful situations

Some people can trace their eating disorder back to a particular stressful event or time in their life. Things that might trigger an eating disorder include bullying or teasing, parents divorcing, the death of someone close, losing a friend, moving to a new school or the pressure of exams.

Physical causes

Do eating disorders have physical as well as emotional causes? Despite a lot of research, no one really knows. However, there are several theories.

There does seem to be a genetic predisposition to eating disorders: someone who has a relative with anorexia is eight times more likely to develop it themselves than someone with no affected relatives. However, it could be the vulnerable personality type that is being inherited, not the eating disorder itself. Alternatively, eating disorders could be triggered by a genetic tendency to be thin or to be overweight.

Chemical imbalances in the brain are another possible cause. Some people with severe eating disorders have low levels of certain neurotransmitters in their brains, and the levels stay low even after they regain weight. However, we do not know whether this is a cause or an effect of the eating disorder.

The brain's chemical messengers

Neurotransmitters are chemicals that carry signals between nerve cells. Researchers are particularly interested in one called serotonin, which makes us feel happy and less stressed when levels are high.

Dieting reduces the amount of serotonin in the brain, making us irritable and depressed and perhaps causing bingeing. Bingeing gives a rapid serotonin boost, leading to a temporary feeling of happiness; sweet foods are particularly good for this. This might be why many people eat sweet foods for comfort when they are feeling down.

There is evidence that a prolonged shortage of food often leads to a pattern of binge eating when food becomes plentiful. This has been seen in people who were starved in prisoner-of-war camps, and in laboratory animals. The bingeing behaviour can last for many months or years. This may be why people who have had anorexia often develop bulimia later on.

Whatever the physical causes of eating disorders, they probably work in combination with psychological and social factors.

Weighing in
Lightweight boxing is one of several sports which lead to an increased risk of eating disorders.

Eating disorders and sports

One group with a high risk of eating disorders is people who are seriously involved in certain sports. For women the high-risk sports are gymnastics, skating, dance and long-distance running. For men they are some classes of wrestling, boxing, lightweight rowing and horse-racing. In all of these, low weight and/or a low percentage of body fat are crucial for success.

According to surveys, between 15 and 60 per cent of girls and women involved with these sports have eating disorders. Another study found signs of eating disorders in 18 per cent of high school wrestlers in the USA. Eating disorders are especially harmful to female athletes because the lack of food leads to a drop in oestrogen levels which, combined with strenuous exercise, causes the bones to become less dense (osteoporosis). Some athletes in their twenties have the bones of 60-year-olds. It is therefore important that sportswomen have a good diet.

Sportspeople are often perfectionists. This gives them the dedication they need to compete at high levels, but it also makes them vulnerable to eating disorders. Coaches can be part of the problem if they set strict targets for weight or

Physical fitness
Eating disorders have been found to be quite common in the US Navy.

body fat, or if they put too much psychological pressure on their athletes. Coaches of teenage athletes need to be especially sensitive to their pupils' physical and emotional health.

Men and eating disorders

Eating disorders are seen as a female problem, but men can be affected too. They account for 5-10 per cent of people with anorexia, 10-15 per cent of bulimia cases and up to half of all compulsive overeaters. The figure for bulimia may be an under-estimate, as men are less likely to come forward and seek treatment. Sports players and men who place a high value on physical fitness seem to be particularly at risk. In one survey of the US Navy, 2.5 per cent of the men had anorexia, 6.8 per cent had bulimia and a further proportion showed signs of disordered eating. It was once thought that gay men were more likely to get eating disorders, but most surveys show that this is untrue.

'Our coach, Dave, was obsessed with body fat. If he thought someone had any flab, he would really let them know about it – in front of the whole squad. Looking back, it was totally out of order. But he had a kind of hold over us, so we'd do anything for him. It really affected the way some of the guys ate and I think it made them feel bad about themselves.'
(Craig, 18)

Research shows that men with anorexia and bulimia share the same characteristics as their female counterparts. They too have an obsession with thinness, dissatisfaction with their bodies, low self-esteem and a tendency towards perfectionism. They carry out the same starving, bingeing and purging behaviour.

Admitting you have an eating disorder is hard for anyone, but perhaps especially difficult for men. They may be scared that people will think they have a 'women's' problem or a 'gay' problem, or worried that they won't be believed. It is true that some health professionals are still not aware that eating disorders can affect men. This means they sometimes ignore the symptoms, or blame them on something else. If this happens, the man or boy needs to find a doctor who specializes in eating disorders and can therefore understand the problem.

6 Treating eating disorders
Changing ideas, habits and diets

There is no easy cure for eating disorders. Treating them involves coming to terms with deep-rooted problems, and with the pressures from society that lead to an obsession with weight and slimness. This takes special skills from doctors and therapists, and is often a slow and difficult process for the affected person. However, most people eventually make a full or partial recovery from their eating disorder.

Pressures
Modern society promotes an ideal of slimness. This is a shop window in Buenos Aires, Argentina, a country with one of the highest rates of eating disorders in the world.

Wanting to change

For treatment to be successful, the person must want to change. Getting to this stage is not easy. The eating disorder is a way of coping with life, and the idea of giving it up is frightening. With anorexia in particular, people often do not believe they have a problem, so they see no need for treatment. They think their low body weight is normal and desirable, and accuse those who want to help them of trying to make them fat.

'It's up to me how much I weigh and how much I eat. Everyone keeps trying to interfere and make me put on weight. I don't want to be fat. I've worked hard to lose weight and this is how I want to be.' (Emma, 16)

Types of treatment

Treatment techniques for eating disorders have improved in the last few years due to better understanding of the problem by doctors and therapists. In the past, most people with severe eating disorders were admitted to psychiatric hospitals and treated alongside patients with all sorts of other mental health problems. This still happens in some cases, but research has shown that people do better when treated by a team which specializes in eating disorders. If the disorder is severe or has lasted for a long time, the person might be admitted as an in-patient to a specialist hospital unit or residential clinic. Others continue to live at home and attend clinic or therapy sessions as an out-patient.

Getting help

Getting help is very important. The more quickly someone receives treatment, the more likely they are to recover completely. If dieting, weight loss or bingeing seem to be taking over your life, try to pluck up courage to talk about it to an adult you can trust. Your doctor or school nurse will be able to put you in touch with people who really understand the problem. Alternatively, you could contact one of the organizations listed on page 60.

The first goal of treatment is to put right any dangerous physical problems. This is particularly important if someone is very underweight. Once a physical recovery has begun, various types of therapy are used to help the person break the pattern of the eating disorder.

Cognitive behavioural therapy is often the most effective form of treatment, especially for bulimia. The therapist works with the patient to help them change their false thinking patterns and beliefs about food and weight. For example, people often believe that if they eat normally they will get fat. Once they realize this is not true, they are able to change their behaviour. The therapist then helps them develop new ways of coping with the situations they find difficult.

Therapy
Therapists help their clients explore their feelings and ways of behaving.

Interpersonal therapy is also useful, and is often given alongside cognitive behavioural therapy. It tries to identify and tackle the emotional and social problems that caused the disorder. The aim is to help people accept themselves and develop a sense of independence.

Family therapy is important in treating children and teenagers. The therapist sees family members together and separately to explore the issues that might have contributed to the eating disorder. Sometimes, without realizing it, the family are actually encouraging the eating disorder by the way they react to it. The family therapist helps them to recognize this. He or she also gives support, because the parents and family of someone with an eating disorder are usually very distressed about it.

Many people find **self-help groups** useful. A group of people with the same disorder have regular meetings to discuss their problems, share ideas that have helped them and offer each other support. A therapist or counsellor usually attends too. There are also Internet chat groups for people with eating disorders.

Treating anorexia

Gaining weight

Some people with anorexia are dangerously ill from starvation by the time they come for treatment, and need to go into hospital. To begin with, someone who has been

Feeding
In extreme cases, anorexics who are dangerously under-weight may need to be fed through a tube passed in to the stomach via the nose.

eating very little will be given a diet of about 1,200-1,500 kcal per day. This is to allow their body to readjust to food. Eating may cause severe stomach pains and a bloated feeling until adjustment takes place. After that they will usually have a high-energy diet of up to 3,500 kcal per day (to compare, the average adult woman needs about 2,000 kcal/day). They need this because people with anorexia often develop a very high metabolic rate when they begin eating normally again, making it harder for them to put on weight. The goal is to put on 0.5-1.5 kilos per week until a target weight is reached. Some residential clinics specialize in treating teenagers and are set up like a family home. The patients help prepare the meals and eat them together.

Eating and putting on weight can be very frightening. The person may feel they are losing the control they have achieved through their anorexia. When they gain weight it may seem like getting fat.

Counselling
A counsellor helps to change a distorted self-image.

Drugs

Drugs – such as antidepressants and appetite stimulants –
are not usually effective against anorexia.

Changing attitudes

Achieving a normal or near-normal weight is just one of
the goals when treating anorexia. To prevent the disorder
coming back, people must be helped to work through their
emotional problems and their distorted attitude to food
and weight. They must realize that being very thin is
dangerous to their health and will not solve their
problems. Other ways of coping must be found. Above all,
they need to learn to accept themselves as people, and to
feel that their life has a purpose and a future.
Treatment is usually based on one or more of the
therapies described above. There may also be
sessions with a dietician to help re-learn
normal eating habits.

Outlook

Some people make a relatively quick
recovery from anorexia, but for others it
is a slow process that may take several
years. There may be times when the person
seems OK and times when the disorder comes back.
One study found that some people needed 3-5 years of
treatment before they got better.

'Family therapy was hard.
I didn't want to do it at first. But
it made us really talk, which we weren't
doing before. Some of the things that got said
were painful at the time, but I think mum and dad
understand me better now. I suppose I understand
them better too. It's helped me recognize some
of the reasons why I stopped eating – to
put into words what I was trying
to say through anorexia.'
(Clare, 15)

Up to half of those who recover from anorexia go on to
develop bulimia. Of course, it is possible to recover from
the bulimia too. Even people who have struggled with
eating disorders for many years can and do break free
eventually. Although they may never be completely at ease
with food or with their bodies, they are able to lead normal
lives.

For a minority the outlook is not good. Some never regain
normal eating habits and their lives continue to be
dominated by food and weight. They suffer from

depression and other mental health problems and find it difficult to form relationships or hold down a job. Sadly, a few are unable to let go of their anorexia and die from the effects of starvation. There is also an increased risk of suicide in this group. Long-term studies show that about 6 per cent of people who are diagnosed with anorexia will die within 10 years.

Treating bulimia

People with bulimia do not normally need to go into hospital unless they are very depressed or suicidal. Most are aware that they have a problem and want to overcome it. Seeking treatment can take a lot of courage because many feel very ashamed about their behaviour.

Breaking the pattern

Treatment is usually through regular sessions at a day clinic or with a therapist. Cognitive behavioural therapy is often very effective. The therapist helps the patient discover what triggers their binges and to pinpoint the negative thought patterns involved. To do this patients

Drugs for bulimia

Antidepressant drugs, especially the drug class that includes Prozac, are often effective against bulimia. They are usually given if cognitive behavioural therapy on its own is not working. People who find it especially difficult to stop bingeing are sometimes given anti-addiction drugs. These stop the brain from feeling sensations of pleasure from bingeing, vomiting or laxative abuse.

People who have been abusing laxatives need help in coming off them, as they can do long-term damage to the gut. They need to understand that they do not stop most food energy from being absorbed. When someone comes off laxatives they may be very constipated for a few weeks and may be prescribed a non-harmful type of laxative.

keep a daily diary of what they eat, whether they binge and purge and how they feel. Patient and therapist then work together to break down the unhelpful thought patterns and replace them with new ways of coping with the trigger situations. They also try to reduce the obsession with weight. Interpersonal therapy – to help resolve emotional issues and improve self-esteem – is often given as well.

Voluntary work
Doing voluntary work, like this girl at an animal rescue centre, can give life new interest and purpose.

The goal is to develop a regular eating pattern of three meals a day; once this happens, the bingeing usually stops. To begin with it might be better to eat six small meals a day to avoid feeling hungry at any time. The therapist or dietician will help patients draw up a meal plan so that they do not have to worry about what to eat or when. They are encouraged to eat slowly and enjoy the food. Occasional binges should be seen as a setback, not a failure. Taking up a new interest or doing voluntary work can make life more enjoyable and help take the focus away from food.

Outlook
About 50 per cent of people treated for bulimia make a full recovery. The rest find that the problem comes back, either regularly or occasionally. This might be when they are under stress or when things in their life go wrong. For some people, occasional bingeing and purging is something that they learn to live with, and it does not stop them leading a normal life. Bouts of bulimia usually become less frequent as a person gets older.

Others continue to suffer with depression and other mental health problems. There is a higher than average risk of becoming addicted to alcohol or drugs. A few people do not respond to treatment at all and become trapped in a daily cycle of bingeing and purging. About 3 per cent of those diagnosed with bulimia will die from its effects or from suicide.

Treating compulsive overeating and BED

Treatment usually consists of sessions with a specialist therapist or counsellor. The goal is to re-establish a regular eating pattern, eating when hungry and knowing when to stop. Compulsive overeaters and bingers must learn to listen to their bodies so that they can tell when they are physically hungry and when they are full. Keeping a diary of hunger and eating patterns often helps. Going on a slimming diet at the same time is not a good idea, as it might lead to food cravings and a desire to binge.

Giving support

People with eating disorders desperately need the support of their family and friends, but this can be hard to give because they often deny there is a problem and push those close to them away. Just being there as a friend can really help, even though the person is not able to show their gratitude at the time. Encourage them to seek professional help. If you are very worried about someone, share your fears with an adult you can trust, or contact one of the organizations listed on pages 60-61 for advice.

Understanding what triggers overeating is also important; again, keeping a diary and discussing it with a counsellor is helpful. Once the trigger situations are identified, the counsellor can help find new ways of dealing with them which do not involve food. Self-help groups like Overeaters Anonymous can offer support and advice on breaking the overeating pattern.

As with anorexia and bulimia, people with compulsive overeating and binge eating disorder need help in resolving their underlying emotional problems. Learning to be more assertive is often helpful, so that they feel able to express their wishes and feelings confidently. Up to half of those with binge eating disorder also suffer from serious depression. For this group, treatment with antidepressant drugs can help reduce the urge to binge.

A message of hope

Finally, here is a message from someone who has been through an eating disorder.

'You can love yourself and your body again. You can get control, get better, and have all the things you dream about having, but first you must give yourself a reason to get better. Each of us can find our own reason to recover, and to quit punishing ourselves. We just have to look for it and decide that we want what it gives us more than we want what we get from our eating disorders. I can't promise you that you will ever be completely free of these feelings and these concerns for your appearance, but I can tell you that life is much better when you open your eyes and see more than the bathroom scales.'
(Reproduced with permission from http://www.mirror-mirror.org/eatdis.htm)

Resources

Books

Bryant-Waugh and Lask, *Eating Disorders – a Parent's Guide*, Penguin, 1999
How to decide if your child has an eating disorder and how to get help.

J. Buckroyd, *Anorexia and Bulimia – Your Questions Answered*, Element, 1996
A guide for sufferers and their families. Covers definitions, causes and treatments.

P. Cooper, *Bulimia Nervosa and Binge Eating – a Guide to Recovery*, Robinson Publishing, 1995
Information on the disorders and the treatments available. Also contains a self-help manual.

A. Crisp, N. Joughin, C. Halek and C. Bowyer, *Anorexia Nervosa: the Wish to Change*, Psychology Press, 1996
A self-help workbook for people with anorexia who wish to change.

M. Monro, *Talking About Anorexia*, Sheldon Press, 1996
Written for young people with anorexia.

J. Treasure, *Anorexia Nervosa: a Survival Guide for Families, Friends and Sufferers*, Psychology Press, 1997

Organizations

UK

Eating Disorders Association
First Floor, Wensum House,
103 Prince of Wales Road,
Norwich NR1 1DW

Helpline: 01603 621414
Youthline: 01603 765 050
www.edauk.com

Overeaters Anonymous
PO Box 19,
Stretford,
Manchester M32 6EB

Tel. 07000 78 985
www.overeatersanonymous.org

USA

American Anorexia/Bulimia Association
293 Central Park West, Suite 1R,
New York, NY 10024

Tel. (212) 575-6200
www.aabainc.org

Anorexia Nervosa and Related Eating Disorders (ANRED Inc)
PO Box 5102, Eugene,
OR 97405

Tel. (541) 344-1144

Overeaters Anonymous
PO Box 44020,
Rio Rancho,
NM 817174

Tel. (505) 891 4320
www.overeatersanonymous.org

Canada
Canadian Association of Anorexia Nervosa and Associated Disorders
109, 2040 West 12th Avenue,
Vancouver, BC, V6J 2G2

Information line: 604-684-2623

Australia
The Anorexia and Bulimia Nervosa Foundation of Victoria Inc
1513 High Street, Glen Iris, 3146

Tel. 03 9885 0318

Internet
About.com
http://eatingdisorders.about.com/health/
eatingdisorders/mbody.htm
A wide-ranging collection of links to sites on eating disorders and related health topics, including chat rooms and bulletin boards.

Eating Disorders Shared Awareness
http://www.eating-disorder.com
Written for people with eating disorders. User-friendly information and advice on all health-related and emotional aspects. Includes links to related sites and chat rooms.

Glossary

adolescence	the years between puberty and full maturity.
assertiveness training	training that helps people express their feelings and needs confidently.
bloating	a swollen abdomen (belly).
compulsive	describes behaviour which is driven by an irresistible urge, often against a person's conscious wishes.
constipation	difficulty in passing solid waste (faeces); the faeces are hard and irregular.
dietician	a qualified person who advises on diet, often working for a hospital or clinic.
diuretics	drugs which increase the flow of urine, causing a loss of water from the body.
fasting	deliberately going without food for a period of time, often for religious reasons.
laxatives	drugs which loosen the bowels, designed to treat constipation.
metabolic rate	the rate at which our bodies use energy.
nutrients	substances used by the body as food.
obese	more than 20 per cent above a healthy weight.
psychological	relating to or arising in the mind.
pulses	lentils, chickpeas, split peas and similar foods.
purging	getting rid of food by deliberate vomiting or high doses of laxatives.
self-esteem	a person's opinion of himself/herself.
self-help group	group of people with similar problems who meet for discussion or support.
therapist	someone who treats psychological problems.
vomiting	being sick (bringing up food).

Index

Note

Photographs illustrating the case studies in this book were posed by models.